THE POWER OF THE OLDER CHRISTIAN

DR. MILLARD B. BOX

"Who satisfieth thy mouth with good (things) so that thy youth is renewed like the eagle's."
Psalm 103:2-5

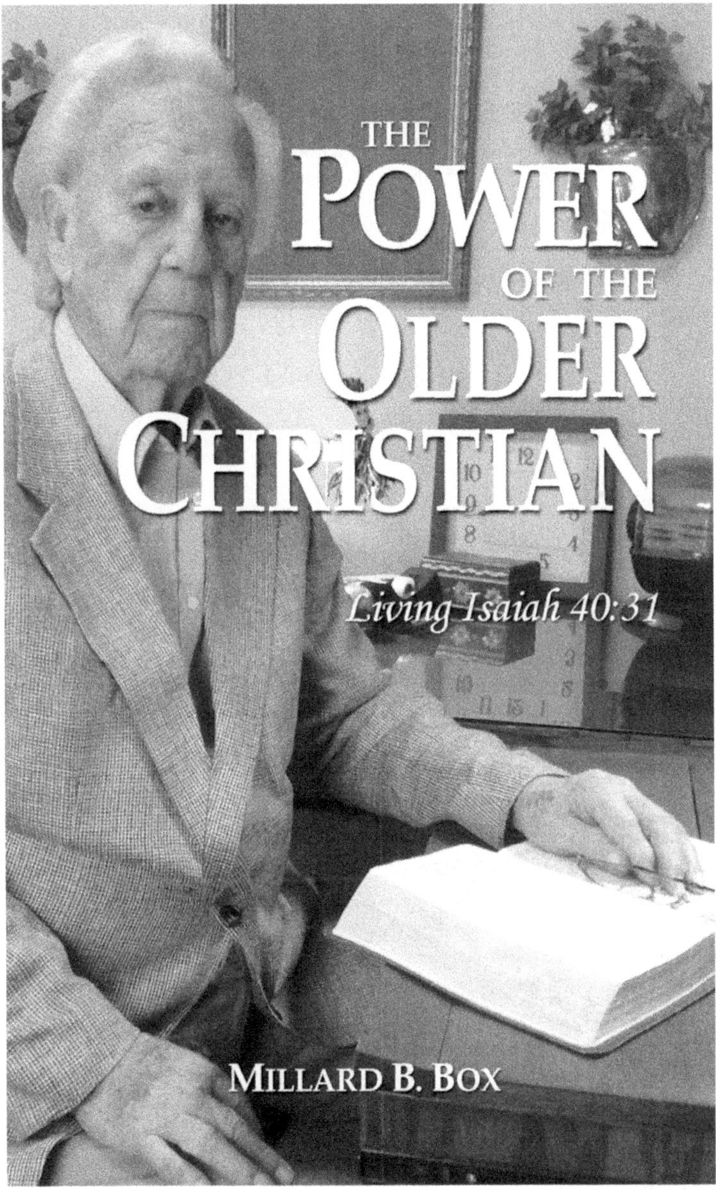

THE POWER OF THE OLDER CHRISTIAN

Living Isaiah 40:31

MILLARD B. BOX

LAURUS BOOKS

Unless otherwise notated, all Scripture references are from the Authorized King James Version of the Holy Bible, available in the Public Domain.

Scripture quotations marked (NKJV) are taken from the New King James Version®. Copyright © 1982 by Thomas Nelson, Inc. Used by permission. All rights reserved.

Scripture quotations marked (AMP) are taken from the Amplified® Bible, Copyright © 1954, 1958, 1962, 1964, 1965, 1987 by The Lockman Foundation. Used by permission.

THE POWER OF THE OLDER CHRISTIAN

By Dr. Millard B. Box

Copyright © 1994-2014 by Millard B. Box

All rights reserved. This book is protected under the copyright laws of the United States of America. This book may not be copied or reprinted for commercial gain or profit. The use of short quotations or occasional page copying for personal or group study is permitted and encouraged. Permission will be granted on request.

Paperback: ISBN: 978-1-938526-74-9

ePub (iBooks, Nook): ISBN: 978-1-938526-75-6

Mobi (Kindle): ISBN: 978-1-938526-76-3

Published by LAURUS BOOKS

Originally published in 1994 by Eagle Ministries, 20358 Northwood St., Fairhope, AL 36532

LAURUS BOOKS
P. O. Box 894
Locust Grove, GA 30248 USA
www.TheLaurusCompany.com

This book may be purchased in paperback from TheLaurusCompany.com, Amazon.com, and other retailers around the world. Also available in formats for electronic readers from their respective stores.

DEDICATION

I dedicate the following pages to my wonderful Lord and Savior, to whom all the glory and praise belong, for His loving me and using me for over 82 years to preach His Gospel of the Kingdom. Praise His Glorious Name.

To my wife, Rachel, who is my daily prayer mate.

And to Stephen B. Box, my son, who is my help in His work.

Judi K. Trimble, my daughter, who constantly prays for me.

PROLOGUE

The information and statements in this book are intended to increase your knowledge about yourself and your relationship with the Lord Jesus Christ. Nothing printed herein is to be construed to diagnose nor treat any individual's problems. We encourage you to search the Scriptures to see if these things be so and to confer with your healthcare professional before changing your eating, drinking, or exercise habits. We do believe we have some good thoughts from the Lord to help you in your hope to live a good, long, healthy life. God bless you as you read.

OBSERVATION

The success of any generation is greatly influenced by its willingness and ability to listen to those who have walked the road ahead of us. To fail in this all important endeavor is to expose the present to needless mistakes and wasted years.

I know Millard Box and have watched him for the greater part of 42 years. Instead of winding down at nearly 98 years old, he is gearing up for still greater days. He deserves your listening ear, and you need his experienced voice and clear example for the best part of your life just ahead, whatever your age.

>Jack Taylor
>Dimensions Ministries
>Indianatlantic, FL
>*[Written in 1994]*

FOREWORD

Psalm 103:2-5 is a blessed passage that ends with, *"Who satisfieth thy mouth with good (things) so that thy youth is renewed like the eagle's."* In the Alps, the eagle lives to the age of 60 or so and then begins to molt, mope, and sit around on a rock. When the storms come, the other eagles fly above the tempest, but not he. Mean, cantankerous, and hard to live with, the old eagle spends his days in mute despair. But, one day, things begin to change, and the old bird begins to care for himself. Scientists, at this writing and as far as I know, have not discovered why this takes place. He gets the cartilage off his beak and talons, preens his feathers, takes on the look of a young eagle, flies above the storms again and lives another 60 years. His strength has been renewed! Isaiah 40:31 has been evident in his life.

This should be true of a saint of God. You are of more worth than an eagle or a sparrow. The Word states, *"But they that wait upon the Lord shall renew their strength; they shall mount up with wings as eagles; they shall run and not be weary; they shall walk and not faint"* (Isaiah 40:31). God will fill the mouth of a saint with "good." God feeds you from His Word daily so that you are renewed as an eagle. The passage in the model prayer *"give us this day our daily bread"* does not primarily subscribe to physical food, although that is suggested, but rather to the meat, milk, bread, and fruit of His Word. Many people die long before their time because they eat "world food" instead of God's "food." Jesus said, *"Man shall not live by bread alone, but by every word that proceedeth from the mouth of God"* (Matthew 4:4). If God's people would consent to be sustained by the Word of God, walk by the Word, and be led of the Holy Spirit, they would not only live longer but also more joyously and fruitfully. They would be excellent examples to the youth today.

I have asked many times, "Who would want what you have if it made them look like you look?" Your face displays your spirit. Proverbs 17:22 says, *"A merry heart doeth good like a medicine but a broken spirit drieth the bones"* (Proverbs 15:13), *"A merry heart maketh a cheerful countenance."* From the marrow of the bones, we are told by medical science, comes the life-giving source to the blood stream. Joy in the Lord shows life. You are a fragrance. Second Corinthians 2:15-16 states, *"For we are to God the fragrance of Christ among those who are being saved and among those who are perishing. To one we are the aroma of death to death, and to the other the aroma of life to life …"*

On the anniversary of his 95th birthday, the old comedian George Burns, when asked if he thought he would die soon, answered, "I can't afford to die. I am booked at the Paladium in London in five years when I am one hundred years old." Bob Hope, at age 85, went to Saudia Arabia to entertain the troops at Christmas. If these men of humor, whose lives are spent to bring a smile to faces just for an instant and have no lasting spiritual value, what in the name of heaven is wrong when Christians can't live that long to tell of Jesus and his love? Most people retire from the corporate world at age 65. Many retire from life at that time. From then on, they exist, waiting for God to "call me home," until they die at 70 or 75. Hogwash! In the Bible kind of life, there is no retirement, and the older a saint of God becomes, the more important he or she is in matters of the kingdom. They should be sought out for godly wisdom and certainly can be the "sweet" to the body of Christ.

We have become so "youth oriented," with emphasis on youthfulness, vigor, "go-get-'em" and "hip-hip-hooray," that we have forgotten that the youth cannot carry the load, either in wisdom or finance or direction. This wonderful enthusiasm will not answer the needs of the church. Of course, we need enthusiasm in our churches. Praise God for the youth and their abilities and "drive." I do not decry that, but I do plead for the faith and wisdom and balance and encouragement of the older saints. We need to see this: If we older ones do not change, then the youth will become like us in the next generation, and God help the world if that happens. There is a great deal of difference between life (Bios) and Life (Zoe) and Life (Chronos). Your chronological age is quite different from your biological age. I know of people who are 50 years of age but look and act as one who is 90 years old. On the other hand, I know of several people who are in their eighties and look and act as forty- or fifty-year-old individuals. The difference is in their life from Christ (Zoe) that keeps them young in spirit and mind.

We have been taught to believe that 70 or 80 is the limit of life, and when most of us draw near that age, our thoughts are filled with dire and dreadful pictures. We make our wills, buy our caskets, make sure we have health insurance or hospitalization, and set our energies to fight our last enemy, death. With the aid of our TV sets, radios, and newspapers, we make preparation for influenza, sleeplessness, aches and pains, and all the dread "infirmities of old age." We confess to ourselves, our families, and anyone who will sit still long enough to listen to us that we have this malady and that ache and those fears of what is coming. When we do this, we get exactly what we confessed and feared, as did Job who said, *"That which I feared has come upon me."* Many of our church meetings are as bad. We fill in the time gaps telling of our ills instead of praising the Lord for His salvation and healing and renewing of our strength day by day. I refuse to go to these sorts of "fellowships" and get depressed.

I read just the other day that an agency taking another of those "polls" has decided that people who are "religious" or who "attend church" have fewer ills than those who don't. Imagine that! The psychological world has finally "discovered" what we Christians have known all along.

We sing, "Like a mighty army moves the church

of God, but the world sees "shuffle, shuffle, shuffle … wheeze, wheeze, wheeze." They attribute Christianity to a bunch of old geezers looking toward an old God that somehow is out of step with life. When the people of God came out of Egypt, their strength was not weakened, and even their clothes did not wear out. They were following a man whom God had chosen. He was 80 years old and doing what God said for him to do. That is called faith in anybody's language. He was not a wimp, a sissy, nor a moaning, wheezing, sickly old codger shuffling along on the sands of the desert, griping because it was too hot or too cold or too windy or too something else. He was GOD'S MAN with GOD'S DIRECTION leading GOD'S PEOPLE to GOD'S DESTINATION. Where were the young people and the children? They were behind him, following this white-haired old goat with his wind-swept beard and his eyes blazing with holy zeal. He was leading a whole nation into the unknown because God had said for him to do it. He had come out of trying times, failures, loneliness, a murder on his conscience, failed self-confidence, and forty years of leading sheep in order to be taught of God and to lead a nation in following God. Here is a lonely shepherd, humble and obedient, with his eye on the distant land of promise, walking by faith, believing his God, and denying himself to please his Lord. What if he had retired at 65, dependent upon the Egyptian government, holding fast to security?

Where are the men like Moses today? Most of us have spiritual Alzheimer's, forgetting the God of today for the traditions of yesterday. We keep talking about the "good ol' days when we were young, Maggie" *(that's an old song, for you young whippersnappers)* and forget that today is our day, *"Bless the Lord, oh, my soul!"* The hope of the future depends on an awakening of the people from 40 years of age upward. We need to have a revival of this group and set an example for the younger people, an example of faith, love, endurance, joy, and the nine-fold fruits of the Holy Spirit.

As you get ready to peruse this book, another thing is needing to be seen. We somehow have the idea that Moses and the other prophets and saints in the Bible were "super saints." Not so! They were people of "like passions" as we are. They prayed, and failed, and prayed again, and sought God's face. But they did not stop! Their muscles ached, they fed crying children, they slept fitfully, and they had major doubts along the way. But since they walked by faith, they continued on, praise God! They believed in change, for God is a God of change. The people who walk by sight cry, "This is the way we have always done it. We don't want praise and excitement and hands raised and laughter. We are comfortable. Don't disturb us. We are waiting to die, you see, and we have retired. Let us alone."

Only about 35% of the people in the United States believe that the church is relevant to their lives. They may be right, unless there is a dramatic change in us by the power of our God. Please read the following pages with prayer. Become what you were made to be. You have a potential not yet reached. For the sake of your own life and the lives of thousands of younger people, live for God, Saint of God, life for God! You older Christians have power to do it!!!

INTRODUCTION

Truth is received in many ways. We believers learn from the preached Word of God, from assimilation of scriptural references, and from personal study of biblical passages based on our previous assumptions of truth (so-called) gleaned from the statements of others who have preceded us on this earthly journey. Much is based on pre-judgment and taken as truth from a doctrinal standpoint without the explicit teaching of the Holy Spirit of God. Thus, it becomes a "letter of the law" without the Spirit and is truly "doctrinal" but not necessarily "truth" as it pertains to what God is saying. In Scripture, it is not what someone says the Lord meant, but it is what He meant when He said it. What someone says the Word of God means produces doctrine. What He meant when He said it produces LIFE. Doctrine is but a shadow of truth. Truth is Jesus Himself and what He meant when He said what He said. If your doctrine or my doctrine does not exalt Jesus Christ of Nazareth as the only hope of mankind, then our doctrine is false, spurious, and the epitome of deception. It is, or becomes, heresy of the highest order and is bred of demonic activity.

The truths that God desires for us to see is revealed by the Holy Spirit directly to our hearts and our minds. He said He would *"... put My laws in their mind and write them on their hearts ..."* (Hebrews 8:10). God tells us in Deuteronomy 29:29, *"The secret things belong to the Lord our God, but those things which are REVEALED belong to us and to our children forever, that we may do all the words of the law [Lord]"* (emphasis added; bracketed words added for clarity). Sometimes these truths come, seemingly, without study or any preclusion on our part. Peter, in Matthew 16:16, is a good example of this. He declared that our Lord was Christ and the Son of God. Jesus blessed him and said that flesh and blood had not given him this thought and declaration, but that it was a revelation from God the Father.

First Corinthians 2 is a chapter that explains, in detail, this matter of revelation. To sum it up, the Holy Spirit is saying that your faith should not rest on the wisdom of man but in the power of God. He tells us that God's plan and method are revealed to us by God (verse 7) and the world wise (religious or secular) could not understand it. The ninth verse states that the blessing of God is upon those who love and obey Him, and God has revealed them to us by His Spirit. The Holy Spirit is the only One Who knows the things of God, and He has to be the One to reveal them to us. These are not secured by human intelligence nor emotions. Read the full second chapter of I Corinthians in the *Amplified* version of the Bible and be blessed to know how God has chosen you to whom He will reveal Himself, His purposes, and His blessings, and,

INTRODUCTION

through you, to others who are hungry for Him. That is POWER-FULL!

The truths that are in this book are for the people of God, to encourage, bless, sustain, and motivate to longer and more fruitful lives for His glory. These thoughts are not based on prejudice, preconceived ideas, doctrinal whims, nor denominational bias. Any person, from any religious or non-religious background whatsoever, who has received Jesus Christ as his or her personal Savior and Lord can benefit from the writings that follow. Our prayer is that you will be one to take advantage of these thoughts that we believe have been revealed from the Lord.

This book is dedicated to the group mainly over 40 or 50 years of age, although any Christian, young or old, would benefit from its perusal. Older Christians are the fastest growing group in America, and this group will continue to expand in numbers for the next fifty years or so. In this vast horde of people, there are millions who do not live a full Christian life as God intended for them. They exist, of course, but they are not "living" in the Biblical meaning of the word. So many are in the bondage of "facts" that are not true, according to the Bible. Satan has led many to misinterpret passages of Scripture so that God's people are in bondage to half-truths or, at the best, have misapplied passages from the Word of God. Even the world picks up the language of the "church" and makes untrue statements that nearly everyone takes as "fact."

Here is an illustration of what I mean. Everyone, it seems, has accepted as a "fact" that a person should retire at 65 years of age, prepare his retirement to reach into the years beyond, but be prepared to die at 70 to 80 years of age. The general populace—religious, Christian, or otherwise—accepts this as a "fact." If you judge by sight, it is seemingly so. However, praise God, there are a few precious folk who shrug such fantasy aside and live long and well, far past the 70 to 80 syndrome. This clan has but a few members at the present time. The idea of dying at 70 or 80 comes from a statement made in the 90th Psalm that says, *"The days of our years are threescore years and ten [70]; and if by reason of strength they be fourscore years [80], yet is their strength labour and sorrow; for it is soon cut off, and we fly away"* (Psalm 90:10 brackets added). The fact of the matter is that this Psalm was written by Moses, not David, to those people in the wilderness who had refused to follow the Lord's direction to go over into the Promised Land. This passage was not written to us at all, except as a warning to walk by faith and not by sight. We will speak of this further under the heading, "The Walk of Faith."

So, we wish to refute the old wives' tale that one has to die at 70 or 80 years of age. We desire to show you that you can live longer than that and do it blessed and joyful, full of Grace and Mercy. It is also true that God promised the youth that, if they would honor their father and their mother, their days would be long upon the earth (Exodus 20:12). How much

INTRODUCTION

more this promise is to those of the children of God who honor and obey their Heavenly Father!

Our prayer is that you will enjoy reading this book and benefit from it. Search the Scriptures, as did the Bereans, to see if these facts be true. Seek His face and not His hand. He loves you and desires to give you *"joy unspeakable and full of glory."* This is our hope and prayer for each of you who hold this book in your hand. God bless you as you read!

GOD'S SECRET FOR POWER-FULL AGING

God has secrets! There are mysteries hidden for ages within the pages of the Word of God. One of them was the mystery of salvation, revealed when the Son of God came to bring God's redemption to mankind. There are other secrets, however. It is so stated in Deuteronomy 29:29. *"The secret things belong to the LORD our God: but those things which are REVEALED belong to us and to our children for ever, that we may do all the words of this law"* (emphasis added).

God reveals His secrets in the "secret place" of Psalm 91:1, *"He that dwelleth in the secret place of the most High shall abide under the shadow of the Almighty."* God revealed His "secret" to Peter in Matthew 16, and Jesus told him that His Father revealed to him that Jesus was the Messiah. In 1 Corinthians 2:7-10 we read, *"But we speak the wisdom of God in a mystery, the hidden wisdom which God ordained before the ages for our glory, which none of the rulers of this age knew; for had they known, they would not have crucified the Lord of*

Glory. But as it is written: 'Eye hath not seen nor ear heard, nor have entered into the heart of man the things which God has prepared for those who love Him.' BUT GOD HAS REVEALED THEM TO US through His Spirit. For the Spirit searches all things, yes, the deep things of God" (NKJV, emphasis added). Note especially that these secrets are given to those that love Him.

Herein lies one of the secrets of long life. We use the Scripture from Deuteronomy 30:19 and 20 for the basis of our thoughts: God said here, *"I call heaven and earth as witnesses today against you, that I have set before you life and death, blessing and cursing: therefore choose life, that both you and your descendants may live; that YOU MAY LOVE THE LORD YOUR GOD, that YOU MAY OBEY HIS VOICE, and that YOU MAY CLING TO HIM, for He is your life and THE LENGTH OF YOUR DAYS ..."* (NKJV, emphasis added).

As we approach these words from our Lord, we pray that His Holy Spirit may give utterance to His truths for your long, power-full life because it is by His grace that we live and move and have our being.

You and I have a choice to make. He sets that choice before us, strongly suggesting that we choose life, and then states that He is our life and the length of our days. It is stated in Acts 17:28, *"for in Him we live and move and have our being ..."*

The basis of all life and living is found in pleasuring Him. In Revelation 4:11, we read, *"Thou art worthy, O Lord, to receive glory and honour and power: for Thou hast created all things, AND FOR THY PLEASURE they are and were created"* (emphasis added). Jesus stated that He always did those things that pleased His Father (John 8:29). If that be true, and it is, then all life starts with Him and ends with Him, and we are here to pleasure Him and enjoy Him forever. So, let us now list the "secrets" revealed to us for a long, full-of-power life for His pleasure.

I

THE FELLOWSHIP OF LOVE

The word "grace" literally means, "to bend or stoop in kindness to an inferior." God has to humble Himself to look on this earth. But we found grace in His sight, as did Moses, for which we praise Him.

Oh, the grace of our wonderful Lord, in that we would find grace in His sight to the extent that He would redeem us and then give us the beautiful relationship with Him that we can fellowship with the God of the universe through His gift of love.

Love can be known only by the action it prompts. The word "love" in the Old Testament (*ahabah*) and in the New Testament (*agapao*) is an active word. It is a verb as well as a noun. *"God so loved the world, that He GAVE His only begotten Son ..."* (John 3:16 emphasis added). The Scriptures inform us that He *is* love. Therefore, His love toward us demands a response—an active, vibrant love to Him and for Him. *"We love Him, because He first loved us"* (1 John 4:19).

This is accomplished in several ways. We are to

love Him with all our being and our neighbor as ourself. Luke 10:27, *"... Thou shalt love the Lord thy God with all thy heart, and with all thy soul, and with all thy strength, and with all thy mind; and thy neighbour as thyself."* Our love for Him is to be unselfish. That is, we do not love Him in order to live a long time. That would be selfish and dishonest, and He would not honor such action. The real object of living a long time is to pleasure Him, to carry out His purpose for you in this life, and to exalt His Name in your world.

Love your neighbor as yourself? Sure! You cannot? He can, through you, love your neighbor, and, thus, you praise Him in a fellowship of love. You love Him by loving your neighbor! God gives someone to you to love you and care for you, and He also gives someone for you to love. He said in Matthew 25:40, *"... Inasmuch as ye have done it unto one of the least of these my brethren, ye have done it unto me."* He gives you power to do that.

One factor that stops the fellowship of love is bitterness. Bitterness is the subtle, secret, spiritual sin that saps the essence of joy and fellowship with God from so many Christians. Included in this activity of Satan are imaginations, memories, hurts, grudges, and anything else he can use to rob you of God's fellowship and joy and life in its fullness. It brings stress and burdens that hurt your soul and cause diseases of the body. We push back into the lower realms of our consciousness this "root of bitterness," and its roots take hold of us in all our living.

Remember the warning from Hebrews 12:15,

I. THE FELLOWSHIP OF LOVE

"Looking diligently lest any man fall short of the grace of God; lest any ROOT OF BITTERNESS springing up trouble you, and thereby many be defiled" (emphasis added). Roots of bitterness defile love, emotions, intelligence, memories, and even the body, much less friendships and relationships in churches and homes. What a terrible thing. This subtle, hellish sin keeps many people from reaching their potential for Christ, and then they die before their time without having known the joy of forgiveness to the full and the deep breath of a burden gone.

I have experienced bitterness in its most horrible attack. After 40 years of pastoring, I was accused of things of which I was not guilty Even had I been, it was not the mandate of mere mortals to judge me. Judging another is a more horrible sin than the sin the person judged commits. When you judge, you place yourself on the level with God, and that is near blasphemy. I could not rid myself of the bitterness I held. So, I asked God to forgive the people for me, since I could not do that for myself. He did for me what I could not do for myself. He saved me from sin when I came to Him, and He saved me, in the same way, from bitterness when I came to Him. I recommend that you come to Him for the relief you need. *"... He is faithful, who promised"* (Hebrews 10:23).

If you have a hurt, a disappointment, a bitterness, an unforgiving spirit toward another, then get that thing to the Lord and get it forgiven now. You cannot be right with God and wrong with your neighbor!

Edna St. Vincent Millay wrote:

> *Love cannot fill the thickened lung with breath,*
> *Nor clear the blood, nor set the fractured bone;*
> *Yet many a man is making friends with death,*
> *Even as I speak, for lack of love alone.*

Love is more curative than most people know. To be loved of God and to love God, to love the other beings on this earth, and to be loved by even a few of them is one of the greatest health benefits known to man. It makes life bearable when it seems unbearable; it calms when fears abound; it balances out the unthinkable; and it eases the loved one into eternity where the greatest love of the Universe awaits.

Agape love—love in the spirit—manifests itself in a self-abandoning gift of self to the other person. There is no selfishness nor self-seeking in this wonderful kind of love.

Phileo love—love in the soul—manifests itself in a sharing of mutual interests and self-pleasing, with a "give and take" attitude that calls for an agreement, tacit or spoken, of sharing mutual interests.

Eros love—love in the physical body—is also a mutual sharing. Here, however, is an ingredient that energizes the older people, as it does the younger. I have seen both old men and old women, seemingly devastated by the loss of a mate, in a short time find a "new and different" love wherein there was spiritual, emotional, and even physical attraction that renewed their lives. I have seen life spans lengthened

I. THE FELLOWSHIP OF LOVE

because of love. Love is so very power-full!

Aging does not lessen or increase love. Aging—and we all age—is not a day-by-day negative life. It is not being born, living a few years, getting married, having children, watching the grandchildren, getting sick, and dying in a few years at 70 or 80. If that is "life," then we are all miserable wretches. This is the reason God sent Jesus to love you and die for you that you might have life and have it more abundantly. Every day you live should be a day of greater love for God and for those around you. You should age in love as well as in years.

You have a choice of where you look for Love. The first place is to our Lord who loves us completely and without question. You can look to the world that basically hates you (John 15:18) or to Him who desires to bless you. In 2 Chronicles 20, the people of God were surrounded by enemies, just as we are. They prayed and said, as recorded in the 12th verse, *"O our God, will You not judge them? For we have no power against this great multitude that is coming against us; nor do we know what to do, BUT OUR EYES ARE UPON YOU"* (2 Chronicles 20:12 NKJV, emphasis added). Here is the Fellowship of Love. Here is helplessness that God desires of us. He loves us so much that He desires us to be helplessly dependant upon Him so He can deliver us. Psalm 145:14-19 NKJV: *"The Lord upholds all who fall, and raises up all those who are bowed down. The eyes of all look expectantly to You, and you give them their food in due season. You open Your hand and satisfy the desire of every living thing.*

The LORD is righteous in all His ways, gracious in all His works. The LORD is near to all who call upon Him, to all who call upon Him in truth. He will fulfill the desire of those who fear Him; He will also hear their cry and save them." He is your power source. Go to Him!

Make a full surrender to love the Lord. Speak it out so your own ears can hear it. Tell Him you desire to love Him as He desires. Do not lean to your own understanding in the matter of fellowship of love. Proverbs 3:5-10 (NKJV) states, *"Trust in the Lord with all your heart, and lean not to your own understanding; in all your ways acknowledge Him, and He shall direct your paths. Be not wise in your own eyes: fear the LORD and depart from evil. It will be health to your flesh, and strength to your bones. Honor the Lord with your possessions, and with the first fruits of all your increase; so your barns will be filled with plenty, and your vats will overflow with new wine."* If ever there was a Scripture that detailed blessings upon one who has a love-fellowship with God, this one does. Just fellowship with Him in love, and you have found part of the secret of long life.

This is your finest hour. Submit to the Lord God of heaven and earth. You will, according to His call of Deuteronomy 30, live and not die; you will be blessed and not cursed; you will be a blessing to Him and to others.

So, fellowship with Him in praise. Praise Him privately and publicly. Worship Him, adore Him, love Him with spirit, soul, and body.

God is saying in Deuteronomy 30:20, *"If you will*

actively love me, praise me in a genuine way, from your whole being, you have thus chosen life, and I will bless you and keep you, for I am your life and the length of your days" (author's paraphrase).

II

THE POWER-WALK OF FAITH

Faith is for old age. The older one gets, the greater should be one's faith. Note the story of Sarah as recorded in Hebrews 11:11, *"Through faith also Sara herself received strength to conceive seed, and was delivered of a child when she was past age, because she judged Him FAITHFUL Who promised"* (emphasis added).

Here is a statement of faith you would do well to learn and speak: Psalm 92:10-15, *"But my horn shalt thou exalt like the horn of an unicorn: I shall be anointed with fresh oil. Mine eye also shall see my desire on mine enemies, and mine ears shall hear my desire of the wicked that rise up against me. The righteous shall flourish like the palm tree: he shall grow like a cedar in Lebanon. Those that be planted in the House of the L<small>ORD</small> shall flourish in the courts of our God. THEY SHALL STILL BRING FORTH FRUIT IN OLD AGE; they shall be fat and flourishing; to shew that the Lord is upright; He is my rock, and there is no unrighteousness in Him"* (emphasis added).

Faith is a gift found in the Son of God. Galatians 2:20: *"I am crucified with Christ: nevertheless I live; yet not I, but Christ liveth in me: and the life which I now live in the flesh I LIVE BY THE FAITH OF THE SON OF GOD, who loved me, and gave Himself for me"* (emphasis added). His Faith is most powerful.

What an outpouring of grace upon us that we have the right, privilege, and honor to walk by His Faith. Marvelous Grace!

In the Deuteronomy 30:20 passage we discussed in the previous chapter, the second phrase gives us another part of the secret for Power-full Aging. He says, *"... and that thou mayest OBEY His voice ..."* (emphasis added). Obedience is based always on a statement from another. You cannot "obey" someone unless they have given you a word of direction, or an order or message. Obedience presupposes an authority and a directive. Faith is hearing that directive, order, word, and doing what He says. Faith without that obedience is dead. James 2:17, *"Even so faith, if it hath not works, is dead, being alone."*

Do you wish to live a long time? Then, heed the words of the Lord in the passage of our text, and not only enjoy the Fellowship of Love, but walk the walk of Faith. Our problem today is that we desire to live long and well, healthy and prosperous, but we do not understand what "faith" is all about. We rush madly on the path of life and get instructions from kindred and professionals, but not from God. Then we wonder why we die so young.

In the Introduction to this book, we mentioned

II. THE POWER-WALK OF FAITH

Moses speaking to the children of Israel in the wilderness. He is interceding with God in the 90th Psalm to remove the curse that made it necessary for every Israelite over 20 years of age to die before reaching the Promised Land (Numbers 14:26-35). They had rebelled against God at Kadesh-Barnea and refused to walk by faith on His Word. They refused the pronouncement of their leaders, Joshua and Caleb, two of the twelve men sent over to spy out the land. The people received the "majority" report of the "committee," believing the ten instead of the two. In this they missed God.

Isn't it strange that it is still true that men would rather follow committees by rationalization and logic, than by the pure Word of God and Faith? If Moses had formed a committee, he would still be in Egypt. In this 90th Psalm, Moses said they were dying at the age of 70 or 80 years because of their refusal to walk by pure Faith in what God said and ordered. The lifespan of humanity has never been 70 or 80 years, and especially those whom God has called. Jacob, who was named Israel, was the father of the twelve tribes of Israel. When he was 130 years old (Genesis 47:9), he complained that he had not yet reached the years of his ancestors.

Moses lived to be 120, and we are told his eye was not dim nor his natural strength abated.

Joshua and Caleb waited 40 years for the "sightseers" (those who chose to walk by their five senses) to die, and then these two old faith-walking men led the children of Israel over into the Promised Land.

These "children" were all 22 years of age and under. Caleb and Joshua were about 85 and 115 years old respectively.

Now do you wonder that men and women die at 70 and 80? They do not walk in love to God and their neighbor, nor do they walk by faith. God help us to see what God is saying to us.

Did you know, older man and older woman, that you are beautiful? There are two reasons for this statement. One, Proverbs 20:29 states, *"The glory of young men is their strength: and the beauty of old men is the gray head."* The second reason is found in Romans 10:15, *"... How beautiful are the feet of them that preach the gospel of peace, and bring glad tidings of good things!"* You see, you are preachers to the youth. You have a beautiful head and beautiful feet. Praise God every moment for that, love Him and the youth, and walk by faith, so they may see and follow you.

As an older person, you are to dream dreams and expect them to come true. Joel 2:28, *"... your old men shall dream dreams ..."* Also, this is found in Acts 2:17, *"And it shall come to pass in the last days, saith God, I will pour out of My Spirit upon all flesh: ... and your old men shall dream dreams."*

I would love for you to capture the essence of the faith of Abraham. God told him he was going to be the father of a son. Abraham was very old. He had walked by faith all the way from Ur of the Chaldees. He had walked at the bidding of the Lord, with the exception of one time when he went down into Egypt. Since God is no respecter of persons, and He blessed

II. THE POWER-WALK OF FAITH

Abraham for walking by faith, He will do the same for you. That grace is sufficient for us today, also.

Here is what God said about Abraham in Romans 4:19-21, *"And being not weak in faith, he considered not his own body now dead, when he was about an hundred years old, neither yet the deadness of Sara's womb: he staggered not at the promise of God through unbelief, BUT WAS STRONG IN FAITH, giving glory to God; and being fully persuaded that, what He had promised, He was able also to perform"* (emphasis added).

My ancestors came from Tennessee and Virginia, before the Civil War, to Missouri. Newly married, driving an ox-cart and living off the land, they faced dangers untold as they made their way west over terrain where there were no roads nor trails. Did they walk by faith? Did they fear the night, the Indians, the animals, and the unknown? Did they ever want to turn back? Did they ever go hungry and thirsty as they plodded westward? I spoke to my grandfather when I was a boy. He told me of a vision of sitting around the campfire at night and reading the Bible and of prayer in the early morning and evening. He spoke of God's promises and their full reliance upon what God said. They were a hardy lot and lived into their 90s.

We live in a wilderness, albeit a different sort, and we have enemies that surround us. To a great extent, we live off the land also. We, too, must be pioneers, and walk by faith in God and His Word. Soft living, however, does not produce this type person. Sacrificial living, on the other hand, makes for great adventure. What does the day ahead hold for you? You do not know. Only God knows. So it makes sense to lean on Him for direction. I believe we have greater enemies than our forefathers had. Theirs were flesh and blood savages, wild beasts and unknown climate. Our enemies are flesh, demons, illnesses, and the world with its allurements, accidents, and a frustration born of hopelessness. BUT, we must face our modern wilderness with the same calm assurance that my forefathers faced. We have the Word of God as they did; we have the same avenue of prayer as they did, and we have His strength to forge forward. "Faith of our fathers" is not an idle phrase. We are pilgrims, the Word tells us, and strangers in a foreign land. We do not know what lies ahead, but we know the One Who guides us, protects us, and cares for us. That is enough! Let us move onward!

Faith is a Christian's lifestyle. You win the battle on a daily basis. There is no such thing as faith for yesterday, nor faith for tomorrow. You can have hope for tomorrow, but faith is for today only. It should be a lifestyle. Paul said in Philippians 3:13, *"... forgetting those things which are behind ..."* Take your yesterdays to the Lord, get forgiveness, and face today with faith. Matthew 6:34 (NKJV) states, *"Therefore do not worry about tomorrow, for tomorrow will worry about its own things. Sufficient for the day is its own trouble."* That leaves you with only today.

Read Deuteronomy 30 carefully, and you will find that God has given you today to make a choice. Choose life or death, blessing or cursing, health or

II. THE POWER-WALK OF FAITH

sickness, prosperity or poverty, mercy or justice, good or bad. Make the choice by faith, and speak verbally your decision. *"For by thy words thou shalt be justified, and by thy words thou shalt be condemned"* (Matthew 12:37).

Work on your faith lifestyle! You do not have to die at 70 or 80 years of age, nor even 90 or 100. When you walk by the seeing of your eyes and the hearing of your ears, you will note people of all ages in all sorts of conditions. You will say, "I don't want to be like that, so let me die early." This is a "copout." God has a span for you to live, and when you look to Him instead of making decisions on what you see and hear, then you can live long and well. Others, both in the Bible ages and since, have lived long and healthy. You can do the same by walking by faith today.

Deuteronomy 33:25 states, *"... as thy days, so shall thy strength be."* Since He is the "length of your days," then He also is your strength for that number of days.

God states in Isaiah 46:4 (NKJV), *"Even to your old age, I am He, and even to gray hairs I will carry you! I have made, and I will bear; even I will carry, and will deliver you."* Hallelujah! So, believe this, and walk in faith. Thus, you will glorify and pleasure your Lord and "live happily ever after." Amen.

III

THE POWER-FULL FRUIT-BEARING LIFE

Here is the third secret for Power-full Aging. The third phrase of God's statement is found in Deuteronomy 30:20, as are the others, which states, *"... and that thou mayest CLEAVE unto Him ..."* (emphasis added). As a branch "cleaves" or "abides" in the vine, so are we to cleave unto Him.

In John 15:4-5, Jesus states, *"Abide in me, and I in you. As the branch cannot bear fruit of itself, except it abide in the vine; no more can ye, except ye abide in me. I am the vine, ye are the branches: He that abideth [cleaveth] in me, and I in him, the same bringeth forth much fruit: for without me ye can do nothing"* (bracketed words added).

Read with me the Scripture prior to this one in John 15:2 and find a truth you need to know if you desire to live long and well. It reads, *"Every branch in me that beareth not fruit He taketh away: and every branch that beareth fruit, He purgeth it, that it may bring forth more fruit."* Do you realize that if a Christian does not bear fruit to Him, his life is shortened? So men are "taken away" at 70 or 80 years of age, or before, because there is no fruit borne to the glory of the Lord. If you have been saved, then you are a branch in the Vine, Jesus Christ. Since that is so, then this Scripture states that if you do not bear fruit, you will be "taken away."

I ask you a simple question: Why should the Lord leave you on this earth, as a Christian, if you are not going to bear fruit for Him?

I was on a trip once when the Lord spoke to me and had me turn to Luke 13:6-9, where the Lord was speaking a parable. He told of a man who owned a vineyard with a fig tree in the midst. For three years, he went to that tree for fruit and found none. He gave orders for it to be cut down, for he said, *"... why cumbereth it the ground?"* Then He asked me this question, "Why should I leave any of my children on this earth past 70 or 80 years of age if they do not love me in an active way, obey me in the faith I gave them, nor bear fruit to me for my pleasure and glory?" What would you have answered Him?

We are here to carry out His will and be the branches *abiding* in Him, *cleaving* to Him, so that His will may be done through us. We are here, saved by grace and bought by His blood to be what He wants and not what we want for ourselves. Full surrender, full cleaving, full abiding in Him, for Him, to Him, and with Him in His desire for us. It should be our desire for Him.

A blessed passage for you to observe is the First Psalm, and especially the third verse, *"And he [you] shall be like a tree planted by the rivers of water, that*

III. THE POWER-FULL FRUIT-BEARING LIFE

bringeth forth his fruit in his season; his leaf also shall not wither; and whatsoever he doeth shall prosper" (bracketed words added for clarity).

Your "season" can be long or short, depending upon your cleaving, or abiding, in Him with your roots of faith deep in Him and the "water" of the Word. If you live for Him and unto Him and bring forth His fruit in your life, the promise is for a long, fruitful, blessed, prosperous life.

Psalm 92:12-14 proves the point above. Read this with me, *"The righteous shall flourish like the palm tree: he shall grow like a cedar in Lebanon. Those that be planted in the house of the LORD shall flourish in the courts of our God. THEY SHALL STILL BRING FORTH FRUIT IN OLD AGE; they shall be fat and flourishing; to shew that the LORD is upright: He is my rock, and there is no unrighteousness in Him"* (emphasis added). Old age is above the 70 or 80 mark, as we will show later in this book. Many are doing this very thing: bearing fruit in old age to the Lord. You can do the same.

God says that, *"The fruit of the righteous is a tree of life ..."* in Proverbs 11:30. You are righteous in the Lord, and you were saved and sanctified (set apart) to bear fruit unto Him and please Him all the days He keeps you here.

One attribute we all need is a "fear of the Lord."

That, in itself, will help you to live a long time.

Proverbs 10:27, *"The fear of the Lord prolongeth days: but the years of the wicked shall be shortened."*

That is an attribute we have almost lost in these evil days when sin abounds. Familiarity with God is dangerous. We come to Him boldly as His children, and He receives us. But this off-hand, brazen and horrible, familiar attitude is a disgrace. God is God, Sovereign and Holy. It would do us well to remember that. In the old hymn, "Amazing Grace," there is a stanza that says, "T'was Grace that taught my heart to fear, and Grace, my fears relieved. How precious did that Grace appear the hour I first believed."

Another attribute in cleaving to Him, or abiding in Him, is hating covetousness. This attribute will prolong life. I merely mention this, but it is important enough to dwell on. Read Proverbs 28:16, *"... he that hateth covetousness shall prolong his days."*

Here is fruit-bearing through your children. Teaching them to bear fruit unto Him is a promise of long life. Deuteronomy 32:46-47, *"... Set your hearts unto all the words which I testify among you this day, which ye shall command your children to observe to do ... For it is not a vain thing for you; because it is your life: and through this thing ye shall prolong your days ..."*

Stay in His Word to bear fruit and prolong your days. Proverbs 3:1-2, *"... forget not my law; but let thine heart keep my commandments: for length of days, and long life, and peace, shall they add to thee."*

The same thought is shown in Psalm 103:5, *"who satisfieth thy mouth with good things [the Word of God]; so that thy youth is renewed like the eagle's"* (bracked words added for clarity).

Set your heart to bear the fruit He produces in and through you. Know that the "branch" does not produce the fruit but only "bears" it. Set your love

III. THE POWER-FULL FRUIT-BEARING LIFE

upon Him and let Him bear His fruit through you. Psalm 91:14-16, *"Because he hath set his love upon me, therefore will I deliver him: I will set him on high, because he hath known my name. He shall call upon me, and I will answer him: I will be with him in trouble; I will deliver him and honor him. WITH LONG LIFE will I satisfy him, and shew him my salvation"* (emphasis added).

There may be one reading these words who feels you are cut off and past "fruit-bearing" age. This is not so, believe me. Pray the prayer of David, as recorded in Psalm 71:9, *"Cast me not off in the time of old age; forsake me not when my strength faileth."* I assure you that He will answer your prayer, extend your days, and bear His fruit through you. David continues his prayer in Psalm 71:18, when he says, *"Now also when l am old and grayheaded, O God, forsake me not; until I have shewed thy strength unto this generation, and thy power to every one that is to come."*

THE REASON FOR LIVING A LONG TIME!

God wants to use you to show how strong He is in you, so that the youth will be encouraged to follow your example of long life and bearing fruit unto God. Show His power through you to everyone who is to come!

Fruit bearing is a spiritual matter. In order to understand just what this entails, we must consider how you are made in the likeness of God. You are a trinity, of course. You are spirit, you possess a soul, and you live in a body. As your body produces the fruit of children, your soul produces the fruit of ideas and emotions, and your spirit-man produces the fruit of the spirit, as recorded in Galatians 5:22.

Compare with me the five senses of the body with the five senses of the spirit in order to see how you are created by the Lord to bear fruit in the spirit by Him.

Hebrews 5:14 states, *"But strong meat belongeth to them that are of full age, even those who by reason of use have their senses exercised to discern both good and evil."* I do not believe the five senses of the body are designated here. No one, without his spirit or instruction of the Lord, could discern the difference between good and evil. I see you with my eyes, but I cannot know by that physical sense whether you are good are bad. The same is true of the other four senses, which are hearing, smelling, tasting, or feeling. I believe the Lord is speaking in this verse of the five spiritual senses named below.

By these five spiritual senses, one may know good or evil.

BODY		SPIRIT
SEEING	*is compared to*	FAITH;
HEARING	*is compared to*	DISTINCTION;
SMELLING	*is compared to*	DISCERNMENT or PERCEPTION;
TASTING	*is compared to*	DESIRE;
FEELING	*is compared to*	RESPONSE

Thus the spirit-senses direct the soul, which, in turn, directs the body. The body becomes the servant of the spirit, rather than the body directing. Remember that the body is the temple of the Holy Spirit, and

III. THE POWER-FULL FRUIT-BEARING LIFE

belonging to Him, having been bought by Him, it must be directed and controlled by Him.

Now, let's break down these five "spirit-senses" and see of what they are composed and how they compare to the five "body-senses."

SEEING OF FAITH. Second Corinthians 5:7, *"... (for we walk by faith, not by sight:) ..."* 2 Corinthians 4:18, *"... while we look not at the things which are seen, but at the things which are not seen: for the things which are seen are temporal; but the things which are not seen are eternal."* FAITH is the eye of the Spirit. You "see" things by faith that you cannot see with your physical eye. This is called "vision" in many places in the Word. So, when you walk by faith, you are exercising (by reason of use) your spirit sense and can discern good and evil.

HEARING OF DISTINCTION. First Corinthians 14:7, *"And even things without life giving sound, whether pipe or harp, except they give a distinction in the sounds, how shall it be known what is piped or harped?"* One can make a distinction about good or evil based on the hearing of the spirit. When one has his "spiritual ear" open to the voice of the Holy Spirit, then the very utterance "heard" takes on a distinct "aura" that indicates it is good or it is from the evil one. Music, originated by the Lord, can be interpreted "in the spirit" whether it is dedicated to the glory of the Lord or not.

SMELLING OF DISCERNMENT (or Perception). First Corinthians 12:17, *"If the whole body were an eye, where were the hearing? If the whole were hearing, where* *were the smelling?"* He is speaking here to the Body of Christ and to the members of that Body. Have you ever said, "I smell a rat"? You were not speaking of the little creature that infests the earth. You were indicating a discernment of a condition that suggested the possibility of something being wrong. Some people have that "sense" in the church body. First Corinthians 12:10, *"... to another discerning of spirits ..."* This person uses that spirit sense in the church life for protection, much as the one who smells smoke in the house and gives warning.

TASTING OF DESIRE. Psalm 34:8, *"O taste and see that the Lord is good: blessed is the man that trusteth in Him."* Psalm 119:103, *"How sweet are thy words unto my taste! yea, sweeter than honey to my mouth!"* 1 Peter 2:2, *"... as newborn babes, desire the sincere milk of the Word, that ye may grow thereby."* This is a spirit desire that compares with the taste of your mouth, tongue, and lips. Sometimes your mouth "waters" for some delicacy. You get hungry for something. The same is true in the spirit. Jesus said, *"Blessed are they which do hunger and thirst after righteousness: for they shall be filled"* Matthew 5:6. The spirit sense of a deep desire for Him and His Word also spurns that which is evil. With the Holy Spirit in your spirit, you lose your "desire" for that which is evil and desire that which is good.

FEELING OF RESPONSE. Acts 17:27, *"... that they should seek the Lord, if haply they might feel after Him, and find him, though He be not far from every one of us."* This spirit "feeling" is the response toward God

III. THE POWER-FULL FRUIT-BEARING LIFE

that comes from the drawing power of God. In that "response" there is such a depth of intensity that the opposite (evil) is known and refused just as that which is of God is received.

Follow this in your thinking and in your spirit, and you will really begin to live, bearing fruit in your spirit and less and less responding to the natural bent of the flesh. As a spirit, filled with the Spirit, you will find life worth living and your time on this earth as beautiful as you can hope. You will age with calmness, security, love, FULL OF GRACE AND POWER!

IV

DEPENDING ON HIM FOR YOUR POWER-FILLED LIFE

Who will live the longest? There are all sorts of papers and magazines on public newsstands today that advocate long life by means of diet, exercise, and the use of certain vitamins, herbs, drugs, etc. Some of these are merely a means of selling expensive publications, exercise mechanisms, or some potent in order to make money. Once in a while, there are some good books and articles to increase one's general health, but you must be very cautious in this area. There is so much "junk" on the market, such as certain concoctions that are supposed to take off fat, increase muscles while remaining in your chair, etc. The basis of long life is not found in science, medicine, or diet alone. Exercise is very good, and I do that and recommend it, but God says, *"But reject profane and old wives' fables, and exercise yourself toward godliness. For BODILY EXERCISE PROFITS A LITTLE, but godliness is profitable for all things, having promise of the LIFE THAT NOW IS, and of that which is to come"* (1 Timothy 4:7-8 NKJV emphasis added).

I suggest, if you intend to depend on Him for your long power-filled life, that you check all matters of health, exercise, etc., with the Word of God and by His Spirit. Let His Spirit and His Word be your guide, and that will save you time, money, and worry. God is your life and the length of your days. That is most important to remember. God is your Father, and the Holy Spirit is your Guide in all matters. That includes eating, drinking, exercising, buying, and selling.

A Christian, by definition, is one that has met the Lord Jesus Christ under the direction of the Holy Spirit and has declared Him to be, by faith, his own Lord and Savior. He has confessed this fact with his mouth and honestly believes it to be true in his heart. Romans 10:8-10 is a picture of this person. He has been "born again," "saved," or experienced Christ in whatever wording you may wish to give that act of faith. I use the word "Christian" in its basic meaning, and that does not mean nor is it synonomous with "church member" or other modern terms for a "religious" person.

In order that you may better realize your dependency on our Eternal God for life and powerfull living, permit me to lead us into some study of our bodies as God made them.

There are three elements in which we exist:

Matter, time, and energy.

MATTER: All things presuppose a Maker. This is so simple that children can accept it when so-called "intellectuals" can not or will not. A watch suggests a watch-maker. Anything as complex and intricate as a

IV. DEPENDING ON HIM FOR YOUR POWER-FILLED LIFE

human demands a Higher Power as Creator. To deny this is satanic, to say the least, for it denies the very Word of God. Man, according to Divine Scripture, was made from the elements of the earth. Two things are evident to prove this, outside of the simple acceptance of God's Word.

One is the fact that man eats of the earth to receive the same elements for sustaining life. Also, when the spirit of man leaves the body of flesh, that flesh returns to the earth from which it was made. I am personally convinced that evolutionists reach their mental basis, not because they are stupid or ignorant, but because they are basically prejudiced against God. Frankly, this is where all error begins. *"The fool hath said in his heart, There is no God ..."* (Psalm 14:1). A better rendition of that passage might be, "The fool has said in his heart, 'NO, God.'"

TIME: The second component of the aging process is time itself. Time is a system, invented by our God, of reckoning duration. God set eternity in the heart of man, but he set man in a capsule of time. Eternity is timeless life with no beginning nor ending. Man was made for eternity in his spirit. His body is in time. Again, time is an element of progress from one point to another. As the days go by, the body ages on its way back to the earth from whence it was made. Time is the calculation of change. It is irreversible. Time itself speaks of God and timelessness.

ENERGY: The third component of aging is the flow of energy. Heat is a form of energy. You are sustained each second by a flow of energy. Food is eaten to sustain an energy flow. Calories are heat energy. All matter bums energy. Metabolism is the processing of food into energy. That produces life. However, there is always waste to be discarded. This is a part of the death process. When Adam sinned, he brought death on all matter, not just humans but all animals as well—everything created. The result of that disobedience is evident. It is so evident that God says the earth "groans and travails" awaiting the adoption of the "sons of God" (Romans 8:23).

The body is fearfully and wonderfully made, it is written in Psalm 139:14. For instance, the lungs dispose of vapors, the skin releases impurities, the kidneys expel waste and parastolic waves pass unused particles from the body. The body is so constructed that it can and does stop bleeding, repairs skin lesions, and "handles" germs that invade the mechanism. Besides that, it has the capacity to repair itself. Yes, you are wonder-fully created in the likeness of your God, living by His energy, in His time-capsule, and for His glory.

You breathe about 200,000,000 times in your span of life. Genesis 2:7, *"And the LORD God formed man of the dust of the ground, and breathed into his nostrils the breath of lfe; and man became a living soul."*

Your heart beats about 800,000,000 times in your span of life. When the Word of God speaks of "heart," however, it usually is speaking, not of your physical heart but of your spirit—not your soul, your spirit. Note what Jesus said in Matthew 22:37 that makes a distinction between the spirit (heart) and the mind.

IV. DEPENDING ON HIM FOR YOUR POWER-FILLED LIFE

"Jesus said to him, 'You shall love the Lord your God with all your heart [spirit], with all your soul and with all your mind' " (bracketed words added for clarity). You use about 40,000,000 calories per pound you weigh in your life span, also. Yes, you are fearfully and wonderfully made.

A mother said to her little girl, "What do you want to be when you grow up?" The little girl replied, "Alive!" That is what we want to be: Alive! Until He calls us to our home in heaven, we desire to live, not just exist.

You may be asking what in the world this has to do with God's Secret for Power-full Aging. Let me hasten to explain that it has everything to do with the way you age. Everyone is "aging." Every child is aging, as well as every older person. We all age. The problem is how we age. What is old? Ask a child and they think someone is old at 20. Ask a 20-year-old, and they think 40 or 50 is old.

Old is a state of mind, a perspective, and has nothing to do with a body. If you think "old," then you are old. There is a great deal of difference between your chronological age and your biological age. You may be 70 years old but biologically only 50. How "old" you are stems from your heritage, your mores, whether you have lived clean or dissipated, your lifestyle, and the "hope" that is in you for long life. The Scripture states, *"Where there is no vision, the people perish ..."* (Proverbs 29:18). This has a great deal to do with your attitude in life and the condition of your mind and body.

Most people age, thinking as the world thinks. The "world" is that system in which we live, whereby the body is utmost in our thoughts, and the spirit takes last place. This is the very opposite and reverse of the mind of the Lord. Note with me 1 Thessalonians 5:23. Paul is speaking here by the Holy Spirit, and is saying, *"Now may the God of peace Himself sanctify you completely; and may your whole spirit, soul, and body be preserved blameless at the coming of our Lord Jesus Christ"* (NKJV). Note the order: Spirit is mentioned first, then the soul, and then the body. We have been trained from birth to place emphasis on the body first, and then, if need be, concentrate on the spirit area. Usually, we end up in the soulishness that governs most of us.

You can age as the world ages—placing emphasis on the body first, or you can age as God wants you to age—living out of the spirit where He dwells in you. Aging is not a downward, dark spiral. Rather, it is an upward soaring of the heart to the Father. Since He is Spirit, He lives in your spirit if you have been born from above, and He directs your life by His Holy Spirit dwelling in you. *Note the diagram on the next page.*

You have no control over age, sex, or genetics. But you *can* control, with the Lord's help, obesity, hypertension, cholesterol, stress, and a sedentary lifestyle. You *can* quit smoking and add years to your life. Read 1 Corinthians 6:19-20, *"What? know ye not that your body is the temple of the Holy Spirit which is in you, which ye have of God, and ye are not your own? For ye are bought with a price: therefore glorify God in your body, and in*

IV. DEPENDING ON HIM FOR YOUR POWER-FILLED LIFE

LIFE DOES NOT HAVE A "PEAK"

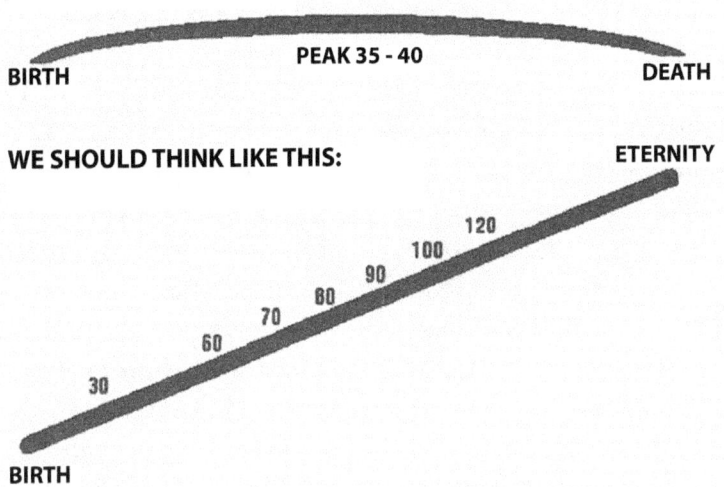

your spirit, which are God's." Eat right, regardless of age: low- fat foods, complex carbohydrates, moderate protein, limit caffeine, salt, and sugar. Decrease calories, increase exercise, and look to your Jehovah-Rophe for healing. It is easier to be healed before you are ill than after you get sick. With this attitude, you will find the blessing of renewed vigor, energy, and abundant life.

You make financial investments for your older years. Why do you not also make investments for eternity? Life is not over when you leave this body. To invest in this life only makes one short-sighted. Wise men get ready for eternity One man said, "1 do not believe there is life after death. When I am dead, I am like a dog. Nothing." Consider this, O wise one!

You are basing your thinking on an assumption you cannot prove. You say there is no life after death. Let us say you are right. I have lived my life for the Lord. You have lived your life for yourself. IF you are right, I have lost nothing. I have been deluded, in your sight, but I will live longer and happier in my "delusion." BUT, if you are wrong and I am right, you have lost everything and will live throughout eternity in a devil's hell, separated from God, heaven, loved ones, and joy unspeakable. Now, consider just how "wise" you are, O wise one. God says you are a fool.

This secret of God—*depending upon Him for your life*—is so very important that I challenge you to surrender to Him now! Again, He said, *"I am your life, and the length of your days."* Please, believe that dependency on Him is urgent for your longevity.

The attitude of the world, for the most part, is that aging is a matter of decline. It is not so! The medical world talks of psychological help. Every time there is a disaster, they call for the psychologists and psychiatrists to come in to help these people in their trauma. Why not call for the Minister of God? They never even think of it. They consider nothing of the spirit of man. If you are recommended to go to a psychiatrist or clinical psychologist, then go to a Christian. There are a few around. They know how to deal with your spirit as well as your soul. You are more than body and mind. You are spirit, soul, and body, as I have stated previously, and as God has stated in His Word.

When a scientist, physician, clinician, psycholo-

IV. DEPENDING ON HIM FOR YOUR POWER-FILLED LIFE

gist, or gerintologist ignores the Word of God, he or she has embarked upon a sea of ignorance of real life and its true meaning on this planet. To ignore the spirit side of a person, and the fact that when we leave this life we DO go to another existence, is to wallow in the sea of ignorance. When any of the above turn from the Word of God, refuse to study it, and refuse to include it in their research, they have deliberately rejected the basis of life itself. When a professional turns to and relies on psychology, physiology, or some other form of expression to explain life and longevity, he or she has missed truth by a million miles. They call this "religion," lumping all groups under one heading that, to them, belies any serious consideration. They cannot understand the Book because they do not know the Author. It is made up of secrets that God reveals only to people of faith, not men of letters. There is a trend today toward "spiritual" psychotherapy. Sigmund Freud, 60 years or so ago, labeled "religion" as an "illusion" and "an opiate of the people." Psychologists follow this false teacher, regarding "spiritual yearnings" as a symptom of neurosis. Lately, they have been changing their minds somewhat. They are beginning to recognize that there is more to a person than physical body, intelligence, and emotions. O, would it not be good if they could come to the truth.

Education, however well-refined, is still eating of the tree of the knowledge of good and evil instead of the tree of life. If there was as much emphasis on knowing God (not knowing ABOUT God) as there is in accumulating "facts," this world would be a better place in which to live.

We have turned to a sort of "rejuvenation" theory in America. The world makes money, selling all sorts of gadgets, exercise equipment, potions, pills, and panaceas to "extend" youth. Failing that, we turn to peddlers of "New Age" and reincarnation, plus a host of other idiotic ideas about the after-life, and completely ignore the infallible Word of God that will never fail nor fall.

Depend on Him for life, for He is your life. In Him, you live and move and have your being. Depend upon Him for life, upon Jesus for eternal life, upon the Holy Spirit for direction in your life. Use all the tools that are given you—suggestions, gadgets, etc., but remember that only your Lord makes it all possible.

V

EXPECTING A FULL-POWERED LIFE BY GRACE FOR HIS PLEASURE

In the beginning of this treatise, we spoke of pleasuring the Lord. I wish for us to pitch our mental tents on this campsite of blessing, so that we may see the full intent of why we are on this earth. Very frankly and to be simple about it, the whole reason for being on this earth is to pleasure the Lord! That, in a capsule, takes in all the foregoing statements in this book. Our duty on this earth is to pleasure our God and enjoy Him forever.

If you choose a full life, living by His Grace to pleasure Him, He has promised to prolong your days. Note Deuteronomy 5:33, *"Ye shall walk in all the ways which the Lord your God hath commanded you, THAT YE MAY LIVE, and that it may be well with you, and that ye may PROLONG YOUR DAYS ..."* (emphasis added).

By this you will see that the Lord desires for us to live long and well, but it is based on our relationship and fellowship with Him, as we noted in our text of Deuteronomy 30:20. On that basis, I wish to lead you in thinking along this line.

There are three segments to life, I am told by medical gerontologists.

YOUTH: 0-20 (Young) 20-40 (Old)
MIDDLE AGE: 40-60 (Young) 60-80 (Old)
OLD AGE: 80-100 (Young) 100-120 (Old)

The Word of God says we are to live to 120 years of age. Genesis 6:3, *"... My spirit shall not always strive with man ... yet his days shall be an hundred and twenty years."* Medical science now tells us that man is so physically composed that he can live to be 120 years old. Set your goal for that figure, living unto the Lord and for His pleasure. He will prolong your life as He said.

Your life is a canvas being painted by you; don't stop until the full picture is displayed. Your life is a beautiful song being sung by you; don't stop the melody before the last thrilling note. There are loved ones listening to you. Your life is a race being run for your Lord; get your "second wind" at 70 or 80, and finish the race for His glory and His pleasure.

This book is not about dying but about living. Growing older is not left to accident or chance. God has your pathway marked out for you. He has even "lighted" it so that you may see as you walk or run. Psalm 119:105, *"Thy Word is a lamp unto my feet, and a light unto my path."* He desires to lead you into "green pastures" and a walk by "still waters."

Aging is not a disease! A Christian has a reason for living. Expectation is a vital dynamic of human

V. EXPECTING A FULL-POWERED LIFE ... FOR HIS PLEASURE

life. Without it, there is no zest for living. Hope and vitality are gifts of God. Hopelessness is a burden from the world.

Your potential, your DNA, demands a full and complete life, for the One who made you keeps you and lives in you. Before you were born, in all stages of development within the womb, you were genetically whole. You were alive in the womb of your mother as a natural part of the reproductive cycle. Your chromosomes, RNA, and DNA were complete. You were there as a choice of one or both parents. Therefore, you are here because of the choice and action of another. That RNA and DNA determined your "bent" as to talent and/or your ability in life to glorify the Lord. I say that because that is why any person or thing is brought into existence. All things were made for His pleasure!

Revelation 4:11, *"Thou art worthy, O Lord, to receive glory and honour and power: for Thou hast created all things, AND FOR THY PLEASURE they are and were created"* (emphasis added). When you were born, you were a spirit within a body with a soul to be formed. Your emotions, intellect, and will were ready to be formed by your parents and the world into which you were conceived. Thus, as God said, *"... you BECAME a living soul"* (Genesis 2:7). Satan, in all his subtle workings, saw to it that you were guided away from God instead of toward Him. Your "bent" was used in any way he could to discredit God. You were, as preachers state, "lost." Then the Holy Spirit found you and called to you to turn to the Lord. Now, you have been redeemed and belong to Him again, fully. That "bent," provided by your RNA and DNA, should become His for Him to be glorified and pleasured. All talents and gifts to men come from God and belong to God. Satan is a thief, so he robs God of all that we are or could be for His praise and for His pleasure and glory. All the talents you see in the world system that are used to entertain the populace and glorify the entertainer belong to God. All music, basically, belongs to God. Satan has stolen and debased much of that talent in order that God may be ignored, forgotten, or hated. Satan hates the Lord. He uses every matter possible to fight our God. So, whatever your "bent" or talent or "blessing," it was given to you for God's pleasure. If you desire to live long and glorify and bless and pleasure your Savior, then dedicate that "talent" to Him and praise Him with that "bent" on this earth. James 1:17, *"Every good gift and every perfect gift is from above, and cometh down from the Father of lights, with whom is no variableness, neither shadow of turning."*

The Social Security system seduces you to "drop out" and make way for the younger ones. Who says so? Today you are capable and then you get up in the morning at age 65, your birthday, and you are now incapable? Hogwash! Many people, after they retire, do not live long thereafter. They feel useless and unwanted. What a pity! They have years of experience, wisdom, understanding of the times, and a life full of memories whereby they can reach out to the younger ones and bless and make life fuller and

V. EXPECTING A FULL-POWERED LIFE ... FOR HIS PLEASURE

richer for them. Life is ever-changing, and there are God-given opportunities to be used of the Lord to bless and help others. Lift up your eyes and look, lift up your heart and pray, and then lift up your feet and go. You have the wisdom, the "bent," the experience, the means to be used of God more than at any other time in your life. Your mid-life crisis is not at 40 but at 60! The older you get, the more power you have from Him to live for His pleasure.

I expect a full life span for His pleasure. Because of this, I have researched the Word of God, Jewish life and manner of living historically, plus Medical Journals, etc., for the material you are reading. My heart is for you, the reader, to pleasure our Lord both now and for many years to come. Hosea 4:6 states, *"My people are destroyed [cut off] for lack of knowledge: because thou hast rejected knowledge, I will also reject thee ..."* (bracketed words added for clarity).

He is not speaking of a general knowledge, as received in a schoolroom, but God-given wisdom from the Word of God. Therefore, I make the following suggestions for you to consider, as I close this book. Your doctor is not responsible for taking care of your health. You are! So, look at these suggestions, pray over them, and let the Lord give you direction regarding what to do. All of these are given so you will live longer, better, happier, and more fruitful unto Him, for His pleasure. Your body belongs to Him, so treat it good for Him.

First, eat right. Many people have diseases and are not well because they have a poor diet. They do not eat the right foods nor do they eat at the right time. They do not even eat in the right manner. That is, they eat too fast, gulping their food. Take time to masticate your food and enjoy the taste of it. Many stomach problems come from eating too fast and while under some sort of stress.

Start off each day with the Lord and a good, nourishing breakfast. I eat fruit, mainly, in the early morning, a good salad at lunch, and then a well-balanced meal in the evening. Eat plenty of foods high in fiber. Stay away from fats as much as possible, and drink plenty of water. In Bible times, they had, generally, two meals a day. They ate a breakfast of whole-grain bread, olives, cheese, and dried fruit. They took a siesta at noon, drank plenty of water, ate fruits, and had a nourishing evening meal. This consisted, in a large part, of lentil stew, vegetables, roast lamb, and dried fruits. They also ate onions, garlic, melons, yogurt, and the like. They ate to nourish themselves. Many of us eat because we are frustrated or because it is time to eat, not because we are hungry. If you will recall, Elijah was fed twice a day, not three times, by the brook Cherith by the Lord. Could there be a suggestion in this story as to our eating habits?

It is recommended that we drink at least eight (8) glasses of water a day (8 ounce glasses), and coffee and other drinks do not count. One should not drink or eat, as a rule, after eight o'clock in the evening, and it is best to make that time around six o'clock.

Stay away from sweets as much as possible,

especially chocolate. Some of us are "sweet-aholics" and just love candy bars, especially chocolate ones. Herein there is a demand for discipline. Eat plenty of fresh fruits, such as apples, bananas, plums, etc. Fresh vegetables are very necessary for the carbohydrates the body needs.

Eat red meat no more than once a week. You may enjoy fish, lean mutton, turkey, chicken, quail, or other fowl. Eat a few nuts from time to time.

Use good sense in your diet, and especially thank the Lord for His provision. The health you have is because of Him, so be grateful to Him and believe, in faith, for good health from Him for yourself. He is Jehovah-Jireh, who supplies all your need, according to His riches in glory by Christ Jesus.

In eating, let me suggest that you be sure to pray over your food and read or quote Scripture at the same time. Read 1 Timothy 4:1-6 (NKJV), *"Now the Spirit expressly says that in latter times some will depart from the faith, giving heed to deceiving spirits and doctrines of demons, speaking lies in hypocrisy, having their own conscience seared with a hot iron, forbidding to marry, and commanding to abstain from foods which God created to be received with thanksgiving by those who believe and know the truth. For every creature of God is good, and nothing to be refused if it be received with thanksgiving; for it is SANCTIFIED BY THE WORD OF GOD AND PRAYER"* (emphasis added).

Second, get plenty of exercise. Even if "fitness" is not in your vocabulary, discipline yourself to some sort of daily exercise, such as walking. This will add time to your stay on earth. Begin, with moderation, whatever you are most enthusiastic about. Take a walk every day, and if the weather is bad, go to the mall. Otherwise, a pleasant day, for me, is to walk in the rain or snow, with protection for my body and my head. Most of the heat of your body is expended through your head, so protect that area. Do aerobics in your home or your office, if you cannot walk. One reason, I believe, that Moses lived to be 120 years old was that he walked everywhere he went.

Increase your exercise program by time and distance as you increase strength and energy. (You will increase in that area as you exercise, so expect it.) The world is bringing in all sorts of exercise programs, selling you VCR tapes and equipment. You do not need all that. Some of these programs are modeled after a non-Christian philosophy based on "meditation," etc., etc. I recommend that you use some good Christian praise music and exercise with someone. There are praise tapes available with good rhythm for your program. You can praise the Lord while you do your exercise. It is not sacriligious to raise arms, sway, and do dance steps while you praise God. This method of exercise and praise is as old as Israel.

A good exercise program will tone your body, increase muscular strength, promote cardiovascular conditioning, and release your anxieties, tensions, and hostilities. You can alternate or rotate exercises specifically designed for your age and body condition. Jay Arnold, Director for Health Promotions and Research Development for the College of

Health and Human Performance at the University of Florida says, "Not only is exercise for seniors health enhancing, it actually prevents certain diseases like arthritis, osteoporosis, and heart disease." He goes on to say, "It doesn't matter if you have never even exercised before; a senior can make the same proportionate improvements in fitness as a younger person." You are never too old to get into better shape than you are now. Exercise! Stretch yourself! Come alive! You will have His grace to do it, and God will be pleased in it!

Third, get plenty of sleep. Ecclesiastes 5:12, *"The sleep of a labouring man is sweet, whether he eat little or much: but the abundance of the rich will not suffer him to sleep."* Worrying over what you have or do not have will steal sleep from you. Casting all your care on Him will not only let you sleep well but will also lengthen your days on this earth to bless others and please Him.

Psalm 127:2, *"It is vain for you to rise up early, to sit up late, to eat the bread of sorrows: for so He giveth His beloved sleep."* A good, brisk walk after dinner, two hours or so before bedtime, will enhance your rest. A short nap in the daytime would do you no harm. Regardless, sleep in a well-ventilated bedroom, use a comfortable bed (this is most important), and darken the room as much as desired. Many people do not sleep well because of an old or too-soft mattress. Be sure you are sleeping well and in solid comfort. Your rest is MOST important.

Do not lie down to rest in fear. David said, *"I will*

both lay me down in peace, and sleep; for thou, Lord, only makest me dwell in safety" (Psalm 4:8). Again, we are admonished in Proverbs 3:24, *"When thou liest down, thou shalt not be afraid: yea, thou shalt lie down, and thy sleep shall be sweet."*

If you watch television, then watch a Christian station or a program that is not irritable or excitable. Many horror stories come through the "boob tube" and are detrimental to a good night's sleep. Counter your fears and nervousness with the Word of God. He wants you to live a long, long time. So, trust Him and sleep well.

Another thing to remember is that you should never go to bed angry or upset, bitter, or hurt at someone. God says, *"… let not the sun go down upon your wrath"* (Ephesians 4:26). Soft, Christian, or romantic music playing as you doze off is a good sedative. If you must have a pill, then take the "Gospill." It will suffice for every night. Read His Word, and place yourself in His hands. You will find life worth living and His presence sweet indeed.

Fourth, maintain a sense of humor. Just as the image of the production in a studio is portrayed on the television screen, so is the real condition of your spirit shown on your face and in your actions. One of the hardest areas in the Christian life to combat is the face that speaks hardness, hurt, bitterness, sadness, or complacency.

To be able to laugh at yourself and your mistakes is an accomplishment few Christians have attained. Christianity is not a long-faced religion! I know that

V. EXPECTING A FULL-POWERED LIFE ... FOR HIS PLEASURE

most religions demand a long face and a serious demeanor. I have seen much, too much, of that. But Christianity is a life of *"... joy unspeakable and full of glory"* (1 Peter 1:8). You love Jesus, whom you have not seen, but rejoice because you believe. This is Christianity: a Person, called the Lord Jesus Christ, is living in you.

Get the anger out. So many carry a "spirit of anger" with them all the time, and the slightest provocation brings it to the surface. The "spirit of gloom" shrouds so many services where I preach. That "spirit" affects the whole service. There should be joy in the services where the Lord is. Read Psalm 16:11 where it is stated, *"Thou wilt shew me the path of life: in Thy presence is fulness of joy; at Thy right hand there are pleasures for evermore."* This is the Path of Life! We *are* in the presence of the Lord, seated at the Father's right hand *in* Jesus Christ. Ephesians 2:6, *"and hath raised us up together, and made us sit together in heavenly places in Christ Jesus."* Now, that should displace gloom and doom, not only in the spirit and the face of the individual believer, but also in the church assembly.

Expect the Lord to bless you each and every day. Look for the positives, the blessings in life. As an old popular song said, "Eliminate the negative, latch on to the positive, and don't mess with Mr. Inbetween."

Look for opportunities to radiate the Lord Jesus Christ. You have a beautiful smile. Use it! I have never met a man or woman in my many years of living that I thought had an ugly smile. A smile is the one gift God has given everyone on this earth. Use yours to bless others and pleasure Him. There is Power in a smile, believe me.

Live for today, plan for tomorrow, and do not dwell on the past. Each and every morning, choose the Lord. Choose life and light and love and liberty; choose health instead of sickness; prosperity instead of poverty; and choose blessing instead of cursing. He bore the curse for you on the tree. God has set this day before you. Choose Him and all He is as He admonished you to do. Choose LIFE! When you do this, you choose to live out of Him, for His glory and pleasure, and you have chosen, maybe without knowing it, longer, better, and a more blessed life for yourself.

Laugh! Satan is defeated, and God is in charge of you and your day-by-day living. You have victory in Jesus and will live today in a beautiful way. So, laugh, saint of God, laugh! There is Power in laughter.

Fifth, depend on others as little as possible. All of us are, more or less, dependant upon those around us for many things. But when you "give in" to a sort of helplessness, or laziness, letting others do for you what you could, with a little effort, do for yourself, you are hurting your ability to live longer and better. Exercise your body, your mind, your love as you go about day by day.

An old song says, "The arm of flesh will fail you, you dare not trust your own." If you desire to live a long and meaningful existence, then maintain as much independence and autonomy in your life as

V. EXPECTING A FULL-POWERED LIFE ... FOR HIS PLEASURE

possible. Do not, however, become so independent that you will not listen to your children, your mate, your family, and others who love and care for you. Doing things for yourself, taking care of yourself, and being active in seeing after yourself is a good way to live a long time. Continue this vein as long as possible. Don't give up, and don't give in. I know people in their 80s and 90s who live alone, care for themselves, drive a car, and even put out a small garden.

Dependency on the Lord, however, is absolutely necessary. *"Trust in the Lord with all thine heart; and lean not to thine own understanding. In all thy ways acknowledge Him, and He shall direct thy paths. Be not wise in thy own eyes: fear the LORD, and depart from evil. It shall be health to thy navel, and marrow to thy bones"* (Proverbs 3:5-8).

In 2 Chronicles 13:18, we read in part, *"... and the children of Judah prevailed, because they relied upon the LORD God of their fathers."* Dependency upon the Lord is an absolute! Dependency upon the Lord is a "healthy" thing. Do not take the statements of physicians, attorneys, or helpful friends as the final word. The Great Physician and the Great Advocate (attorney) has the final word about you, your body, your living, and your extent of life. Listen to their advice and counsel and then bring those ideas and statements to the Lord who *"is your life and the length of your days."*

Sixth in our suggestions, make yourself necessary to others. As you proceed in your independence as much as possible, be sure to make yourself necessary to others. You are a child of God, made by Him, saved by Him, and placed by Him where you are now at this time to carry out a specified work for His pleasure and for His glory. You are necessary to the Lord and to others. Begin to think that way.

Be responsible for others. Help someone else to achieve greatness in the eyes of the Lord. Many are struggling to know who they are and why they are here. They have never identified themselves as His children, and they need to know who they are in Christ. You can help them.

Again, think on the fact that there are many young people, and some children, who do not have a daddy or a mama. They have a father and a mother (necessary fact of birth), but many are alienated for one reason or the other, and they need someone to love them. I am a "daddy" and "granddad" to many younger people across this nation. They have turned to me because they have no one to love them in that capacity. They know that I love them because of the love of Christ in me. I have no "agenda" or "axe to grind" in our relationships. I merely love them because they need to be loved. It is that simple. Paul described this matter in 1 Corinthians 4:15, *"For though ye have ten thousand instructors in Christ, yet have ye not many fathers: for in Christ Jesus I have begotten you through the Gospel."* Be a "daddy" or a "mother" to some younger man or woman, and find your life being renewed with purpose and energy you have not experienced before. They need your love, your experience, and your wisdom. You are

V. EXPECTING A FULL-POWERED LIFE ... FOR HIS PLEASURE

necessary. Believe it! Act on it! Pleasure God in the loving of others as He pleases you in loving you.

Seventh suggestion is that you don't slow down. You will hear older people tell you, "You're getting old. Better slow down." Don't do it! Don't slow down. If your body slows a bit, that is natural. It will tell you how "fast" to go, but don't slow down in your spirit and your soul. Think young, think for tomorrow, and think of what God is desiring to do with you for His glory. There is nothing in the Word of God that suggests, as far as I know, that you must slow down as you get older.

One older man said to a pastor, when I was in a meeting in a church, "Isn't it time for Box to hang up his sword?" The young pastor replied, "Man, he is just now beginning his work. He will never hang up the Sword of the Spirit until God calls Him home." Good answer! Moses spent 40 years in Egypt, 40 years in the desert and when he was 80 years old, he began his life work for which he had been prepared. He led God's people out of bondage after two-thirds of his life span was over. At 80 years of age, he did what God had called him to do as a young man. Why should you give up at your age? There is much work to do, and God never told you to turn over your mantle to someone else. You have Power to continue in His purpose for you.

A fear of dying, a giving in to the aches and pains, a surrender to the mental attitude that one is too old will let you die younger than was meant to be. A fear of the future, or a fear of sickness, or of being a burden to someone will cause you to slow down and prevent the fulfillment of God's purpose in your life. Proverbs 3:25, *"Be not afraid of sudden fear ..."* Don't be afraid of a sudden malady such as a heart attack or stroke. Fear does not help you. It hurts you. If you are under a doctor's care, do what he says, but do not live in fear.

Believe God to be your Great Physician, your Jehovah-Rophe, healing you, caring for you, and sustaining you daily and hourly. Look to Him each moment as little situations happen in your body, and believe Him to be healing you. He is your Life, and the length of your days. In Him you live and move and have your being. Set your goal to live to be 120 years old as a witness of the goodness of the Lord. Plan on every day in every year to be dedicated to pleasing and glorifying Him. One physician calls it "self-efficacy." He means that as you set your mind to live, you will live. As your spirit is, so you think. As you think, you speak. As you speak, so it is. Matthew 12:37, *"For by thy words thou shalt be justfied, and by thy words thou shalt be condemned."* You speak what you think out of your spirit. So, speak life and love and praise to the Lord who loves you and keeps you. Proverbs 17:22 says, *"A merry heart doeth good like a medicine ..."* I repeat what I said before. If George Burns could live to 95 or so to make people laugh and escape reality for a few minutes, surely you can live as long or longer to witness of the love and care of your heavenly Father and bring people to Him. Entertainers fill our world. They bring amusement to people. That word, "amusement" comes from two Greek words that mean "not to think." Entertainment diverts one's mind for a moment so we do not think of our state or condition. But, a life lived for the glory of the Lord turns men to face eternity and praise God through the ages for His goodness. Don't be an entertainer, but be an enabler.

CONCLUSION

In considering all the relative Scriptures and the need of the older ones who may read this book; considering the aspect of those that are ill, incapacitated, or suffering hindrances to a full, active life; looking to the basic intent of the Word of God, then I wish to assert that, in all situations, we are to love Him, look to Him, give Him praise, and if not able to understand all our situations, to trust Him because He loves every one of us. He is the Lord and knows all things perfectly. I may not live to be 100 or 120, but I will live longer for Him than if I set my goal for 70 or 80. It is really not how long I live, but the quality of my life as I live.

To live selfishly for myself or even for close kindred; to just live because I am here; to exist because I exist; to live to "make a living" or "raise a family"; or any other of a million reasons for living, is not justifiable in view of eternity and the One Who died for me on the Cross of Calvary. I am to live for Him, unto Him, and because of Him. I am to live for

His sake and for His pleasure and to do His will. I am His, bought by His blood, living by His grace, and breathing by His mercy. He is Wonderful and Mighty and Exalted. He is my life and my love. So, because of this, I give you these thoughts. My desire is to broaden your horizons, lift your spirit, help you set new goals, and bring you to the very essence of life, *"... which is Christ in you, the hope of glory!"* (Colossians 1:27).

We wish to help you to live as long as God wants you to live; to live as much in full health as possible; to live as unselfishly as you can, as joyously as you desire, and for you to bring Him as much glory and praise as any human can do in this life. God bless you and keep you and love you is our prayer for you now and always. You can live a POWER-FULL life for His glory. Do it! Amen.

ABOUT THE AUTHOR

DR. MILLARD B. BOX

Dr. Millard B. Box, at the age of 97, has refused to retire. He has been preaching for 82 years, with 40 years as a Southern Baptist pastor.

Robust and healthy at his age, he is an encouraging figure for an example of the truth of his book, *The Power of the Older Christian*. Written over 20 years ago, this book is an encouragment to young and old alike. You will be touched by the wisdom and experience gained by this man from over eight decades of service to his Lord Jesus Christ.

Dr. Box travels both in the United States and foreign countries upon invitation. He and his wife, Rachel, reside in Fairhope, Alabama.

NOTES

NOTES

www.ingramcontent.com/pod-product-compliance
Lightning Source LLC
Chambersburg PA
CBHW060851050426
42453CB00008B/934